My State
NEW YORK

By Christina Earley

TABLE OF CONTENTS

A Crabtree Seedlings Book

Crabtree Publishing
crabtreebooks.com

T0414156

School-to-Home Support for Caregivers and Teachers

This book helps children grow by letting them practice reading. Here are a few guiding questions to help the reader build his or her comprehension skills. Possible answers appear in red.

Before Reading:

• What do I know about New York?
  • *I know that New York is a state.*
  • *I know that New York is near two of the Great Lakes.*

• What do I want to learn about New York?
  • *I want to learn which famous people were born in New York.*
  • *I want to learn what the state flag looks like.*

During Reading:

• What have I learned so far?
  • *I have learned that Albany is the state capital of New York.*
  • *I have learned that 3,160 tons (2,867 metric tons) of water go over Niagara Falls every second.*

• I wonder why...
  • *I wonder why the state flower is the rose.*
  • *I wonder why there are castles in the Thousand Islands.*

After Reading:

• What did I learn about New York?
  • *I have learned that Lake Placid has a bobsled track.*
  • *I have learned that the state animal is the beaver.*

• Read the book again and look for the glossary words.
  • *I see the word **capital** on page 6, and the word **legend** on page 18. The other glossary words are found on pages 22 and 23.*

I live in New York City. The **skyscrapers** here are very tall.

My city has the first-ever pizzeria in the United States.

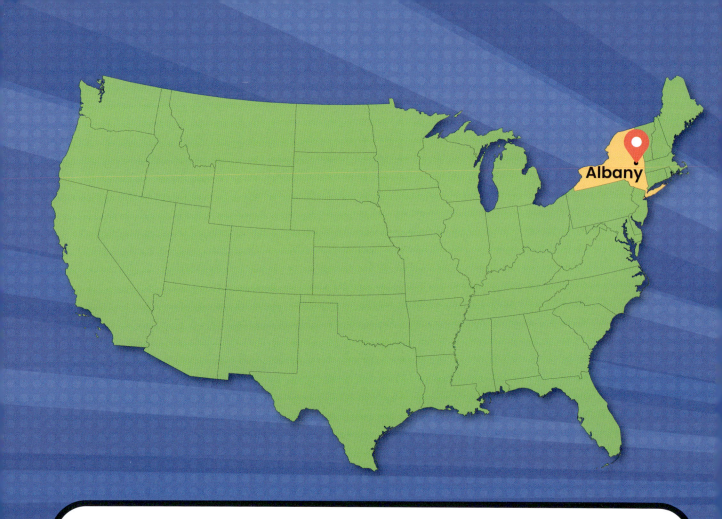

New York is in the northeastern United States. The **capital** is Albany.

Fun Fact: New York City is the largest city in the state of New York.

The state animal is the **beaver**.

We grow a lot of apples. Some of them are used to make my favorite dessert, apple pie!

Fun Fact: New York is one of the states that grows the most apples in the U.S.

My state flag has a **shield** on it. The shield shows boats on the Hudson River.

There are 12 national sports teams in New York.

I like to visit Niagara Falls State Park. There is a boat tour that gets close to the roaring water.

Fun Fact: More than 3,160 tons (2,867 metric tons) of water go over Niagara Falls every second.

There are some castles to see by boat in the Thousand Islands.

I ride the roller coasters at Coney Island.

Rap artist Jay-Z was born in New York. NBA **legend** Michael Jordan was also born in New York.

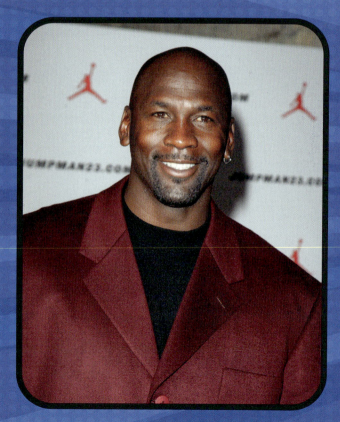

Fun Fact: Sonia Sotomayor, who serves on the Supreme Court of the United States, was born in the Bronx, New York.

I sled on a **bobsled** track in Lake Placid.

CURVE 14

I ride on a horse at the Herschell Carrousel Factory Museum.

Glossary

 **beaver** (bee-ver): A small animal that has thick, brown fur and a wide, flat tail, and lives both on land and in water

 **bobsled** (bob-sled): A sled for two or four people that slides over ice and snow and is used for racing

 **capital** (cap-ih-tuhl): The city or town where the government of a country, state, or province is located

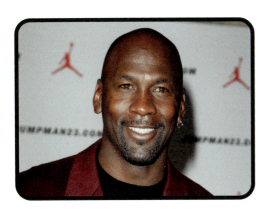

legend (leh-jind): A very famous person who is known for doing something well

shield (sheeld): A picture that is shaped like a soldier's shield

skyscrapers (skie-skray-perz): Very tall buildings

Index

Written by: Christina Earley
Designed and Illustrated by: Bobbie Houser
Series Development: James Earley
Proofreader: Melissa Boyce
Educational Consultant: Marie Lemke M.Ed.

About the Author

Christina Earley lives in sunny South Florida with her husband and son. She enjoys traveling around the United States and learning about different historical places. Her hobbies include hiking, yoga, and baking.

Photographs:
Alamy: Ieronymos: p. 5; Max Simson: p. 14-15; WDC Photos: p. 19; Philip Scalia: p. 21
Shutterstock: spyarm: cover; Mihai_Andritoiu: p. 3; Taiga: p. 4, 23; Volina: p. 6, 22; Sean Pavone: p. 7; Christian Musat: p. 8, 22; ER_09: p. 9; jewelspics: p. 10-11; 5 second Studio: p. 11; Wangkun Jia: p. 12, 23; Debby Wong: p. 13, 18 left; Jam Norasett: p. 15; Elenarts: p. 16; James Kirkikis: p. 17; landmarkmedia: p. 18 right, 23; Steve Broer: p. 20, 22

Crabtree Publishing

crabtreebooks.com   800-387-7650
Copyright © 2023 Crabtree Publishing

Printed in the U.S.A./012023/CG20220815

Published in Canada
Crabtree Publishing
616 Welland Avenue
St. Catharines, Ontario
L2M 5V6

Published in the United States
Crabtree Publishing
347 Fifth Avenue
Suite 1402-145
New York, New York, 10016

Library and Archives Canada Cataloguing in Publication
Available at Library and Archives Canada

Library of Congress Cataloging-in-Publication Data
Available at the Library of Congress

Hardcover: 978-1-0396-9658-7
Paperback: 978-1-0396-9765-2
Ebook (pdf): 978-1-0396-9979-3
Epub: 978-1-0396-9872-7